# A MUSICAL JOURNEY
## EPISODES I–VI
### INSTRUMENTAL SOLOS

Music by JOHN WILLIAMS

D1539481

## CONTENTS

© 2009 Alfred Publishing Co., Inc.
All Rights Reserved. Printed in USA.

Alfred

ISBN-10: 0-7390-5829-0
ISBN-13: 978-0-7390-5829-9

Arranged by Bill Galliford, Ethan Neuburg and Tod Edmondson

# STAR WARS
## (Main Theme)

Music by
**JOHN WILLIAMS**

**Majestically, steady march (♩ = 108)**

Star Wars - 5 - 1
32131

4

6

# JAR JAR'S INTRODUCTION

By
**JOHN WILLIAMS**

**Moderately (♩ = 80)**

*(Tempo click)*

Jar Jar's Introduction - 3 - 1
32131

# AUGIE'S GREAT MUNICIPAL BAND

By
**JOHN WILLIAMS**

**Joyously** (♩ = 126)

Augie's Great Municipal Band - 4 - 1
32131

**33**

# QUI-GON'S FUNERAL

By<br>JOHN WILLIAMS

**Dirge, solemnly (♩ = 60)**

Qui-Gon's Funeral - 2 - 1
32131

# DUEL OF THE FATES

Music by
**JOHN WILLIAMS**

Duel of the Fates - 8 - 1
32131

18

Duel of the Fates - 8 - 3
32131

Duel of the Fates - 8 - 6
32131

# ANAKIN'S THEME

By
**JOHN WILLIAMS**

**Moderato ($\quad$ = 76)**

*(Tempo click)*

Anakin's Theme - 4 - 1
32131

**15**

# THE FLAG PARADE

By
**JOHN WILLIAMS**

**Majestically (♩ = 92)**
*(Tempo click)*

The Flag Parade - 5 - 1
32131

# THE ARENA

Music by
**JOHN WILLIAMS**

The Arena - 5 - 1
32131

34

# CONTENTS

Arranged by Bill Galliford, Ethan Neuburg and Tod Edmondson

ISBN-10: 0-7390-5829-0
ISBN-13: 978-0-7390-5829-9

4

# STAR WARS
### (Main Theme)

Music by
**JOHN WILLIAMS**

**Majestically, steady march (♩ = 108)**

# JAR JAR'S INTRODUCTION

By
**JOHN WILLIAMS**

# AUGIE'S GREAT MUNICIPAL BAND

By
JOHN WILLIAMS

# QUI-GON'S FUNERAL

By
**JOHN WILLIAMS**

# DUEL OF THE FATES

Music by
**JOHN WILLIAMS**

# ANAKIN'S THEME

By
JOHN WILLIAMS

Anakin's Theme - 2 - 1
32131

# THE FLAG PARADE

By
**JOHN WILLIAMS**

The Flag Parade - 2 - 1
32131

# THE ARENA

Music by
**JOHN WILLIAMS**

The Arena - 2 - 1
32131

15

The Arena - 2 - 2
32131

# ACROSS THE STARS
## (Love Theme from *STAR WARS*®: EPISODE II)

Music by
**JOHN WILLIAMS**

Across the Stars - 2 - 1
32131

# THE MEADOW PICNIC

Music by
**JOHN WILLIAMS**

# THE IMPERIAL MARCH
### (Darth Vader's Theme)

Music by
**JOHN WILLIAMS**

# BATTLE OF THE HEROES

(From *Star Wars*®: Episode III *Revenge of the Sith*)

Music by
**JOHN WILLIAMS**

Battle of the Heroes - 2 - 1
32131

# CANTINA BAND

Music by
**JOHN WILLIAMS**

**Moderately fast ragtime** ($\quad$ = 112)

*To Coda* ⊕

Cantina Band - 2 - 1
32131

# THE THRONE ROOM

Music by
**JOHN WILLIAMS**

\* E♯ = F♮

\*\* B♯ = C♮

The Throne Room - 2 - 1
32131

# MAY THE FORCE BE WITH YOU

Music by
**JOHN WILLIAMS**

# PRINCESS LEIA'S THEME

Music by
**JOHN WILLIAMS**

Moderately slow, with a gentle flow (♩ = 72)

# STAR WARS

## A MUSICAL JOURNEY
### EPISODES I–VI
INSTRUMENTAL SOLOS

This book is part of a string series arranged for Violin, Viola and Cello. The arrangements are completely compatible with each other and can be played together or as solos. Each book features a specially designed piano accompaniment that can be easily played by a teacher or intermediate piano student, as well as a carefully crafted removable part, complete with bowings, articulations and keys well suited for the Level 2–3 player. A fully orchestrated accompaniment CD is also provided. The CD includes a DEMO track of each song, which features a live string performance, followed by a PLAY-ALONG track.

This book is also part of a *Star Wars*®: A Musical Journey (Episodes I–VI) Instrumental Solo series written for Flute, Clarinet, alto Sax, Tenor Sax, Trumpet, Horn in F and Trombone. An orchestrated accompaniment CD is included. A **piano accompaniment** book (optional) is also available. Due to level considerations regarding keys and instrument ranges, the arrangements in the **wind instrument** series are not compatible with those in the **string instrument** series.

The Arena - 5 - 5
32131

# ACROSS THE STARS
### (Love Theme from *STAR WARS*®: EPISODE II)

Music by
**JOHN WILLIAMS**

**Moderately slow & gently** (♩ = 76)

*(with pedal)*

# THE MEADOW PICNIC

Music by
**JOHN WILLIAMS**

**Moderately slow and flowing (♩. = 50)**

The Meadow Picnic - 3 - 1
32131

**28**

**33**

**37**

poco rit. e dim.

mp

poco rit. e dim.

mp

* E# = F♮

# THE IMPERIAL MARCH
## (Darth Vader's Theme)

Music by
**JOHN WILLIAMS**

**March style (♩ = 108)**
*(Tempo click)*

The Imperial March - 3 - 1
32131

**49**

The Imperial March - 3 - 3
32131

# BATTLE OF THE HEROES

(From *Star Wars*®: Episode III *Revenge of the Sith*)

Music by
**JOHN WILLIAMS**

Battle of the Heroes - 8 - 1
32131

54

# CANTINA BAND

Music by
**JOHN WILLIAMS**

**Moderately fast ragtime (♩ = 112)**

Cantina Band - 4 - 1
32131

Cantina Band - 4 - 2
32131

60

Cantina Band - 4 - 3
32131

D.S. 𝄋 al Coda

⊕ Coda

Cantina Band - 4 - 4
32131

# THE THRONE ROOM

Music by
**JOHN WILLIAMS**

**Maestoso** (♩ = 112)

\*E♯ = F♮

\*\*B♯ = C♮

The Throne Room - 4 - 1
32131

# MAY THE FORCE BE WITH YOU

Music by
**JOHN WILLIAMS**

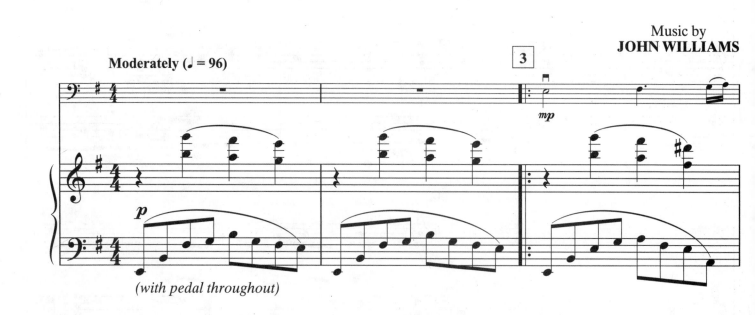

*(with pedal throughout)*

May the Force Be With You - 3 - 1
32131

May the Force Be With You - 3 - 2
32131

# PRINCESS LEIA'S THEME

Music by
**JOHN WILLIAMS**

**Moderately slow, with a gentle flow (♩ = 72)**

*(with pedal)*

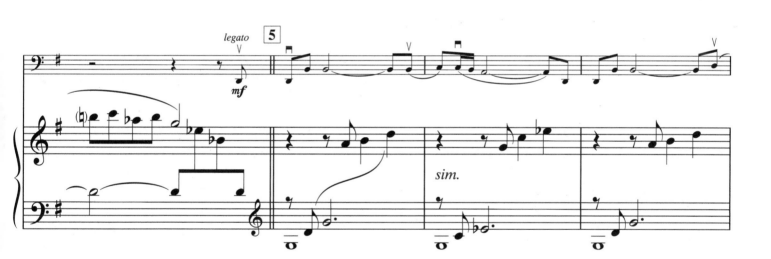

Princess Leia's Theme - 3 - 1
32131

70